The Super Easy

CROCK POT

COOKBOOK 2024

Lisa Larsen

Copyright Notice

CONTENTS

INTRODUCTION

Welcome to "The Super Easy Crock Pot Cookbook 2024," your essential guide to transforming everyday meals into effortless gourmet experiences. Whether you're a seasoned home cook or new to the culinary world, this cookbook is designed to simplify your life and enhance your meals with delicious, healthy, and easy recipes that can be prepared in a crock pot.

In today's fast-paced world, finding time to cook nutritious meals can be a challenge. That's where your crock pot comes in—a versatile kitchen tool that makes meal preparation as simple as adding ingredients and setting the timer. This book will take you on a culinary journey, providing over 2000 days of recipes that range from morning breakfasts to late-night desserts, all tailored to be both simple and nutritious.

But this book is more than just a collection of recipes. It's a comprehensive guide to mastering slow cooking, with full-color pictures to inspire you and a 4-week meal plan to get you started. Each recipe has been meticulously developed to ensure it's not only healthy and easy to make but also bursting with flavor.

Throughout these pages, you'll discover:

Practical Tips for Crock Pot Mastery: From selecting the right crock pot to essential kitchen tools and ingredients.

A Variety of Recipes: Catering to all tastes and dietary needs, including vegetarian and gluten-free options.

Time-Saving Techniques: How to maximize your crock pot's potential, making cooking more efficient than ever.

Nutritional Information: To help you maintain a balanced diet while enjoying delicious meals.

This cookbook is your ticket to reclaiming time—time to spend with family, time for yourself, and time to enjoy good food without the stress of daily meal preparation. Whether you're looking to impress guests, feed your family, or just treat yourself to a tasty meal, "The Super Easy Crock Pot Cookbook 2024" will be your go-to resource for making wholesome meals with minimal effort.

So, dust off your crock pot, gather your ingredients, and prepare to transform the way you cook. Let's make every meal an effortless celebration of flavor and health! "The Super Easy Crock Pot Cookbook 2024", designed to provide readers with a solid foundation for using their crock pot effectively and safely.

CHAPTER 1
Getting Started with Your Crock Pot

What is a Crock Pot?

A crock pot, also commonly referred to as a slow cooker, is a countertop electrical cooking appliance used to simmer at a lower temperature than other cooking methods, such as boiling, baking, and frying. This allows for unattended cooking for many hours of dishes that would otherwise be boiled: pot roast, soups, stews, and other dishes (including beverages, desserts, and dips).

Types of Crock Pots

(1) **Basic Crock Pots:** These models have a simple low and high cooking setting without a timer or programmable features.

(2) **Programmable Crock Pots:** These come with multiple cooking settings, including a timer and sometimes a keep-warm function, allowing for greater control over cooking times and temperatures.

(3) **Multi-Cookers:** These versatile appliances combine the functions of a crock pot with those of a pressure cooker, rice cooker, steamer, and sometimes even an air fryer, offering a comprehensive solution for all cooking needs.

Choosing the Best Model

For Busy Individuals: Programmable crock pots that can switch to a warm setting after cooking are ideal.

For Large Families: Look for larger models that can accommodate bigger portions.

For Singles or Couples: Smaller models are sufficient and take up less space.

Essential Tools and Ingredients: Guide to Must-Have Kitchen Tools and Pantry Staples for Crock Pot Cooking

Tools

Meat Thermometer: Ensures meats are cooked safely to the right temperature.

Kitchen Tongs: Useful for removing hot items safely.

Ladle: Perfect for serving soups and stews.

Cutting Board and Knives: Essential for prep work.

Pantry Staples

Broths and Stocks: Provide flavor bases for countless dishes.

Dried Herbs and Spices: Enhance the flavor of slow-cooked meals.

Canned Vegetables and Beans: Handy and time-saving for adding substance.

Whole Grains: Such as rice or quinoa, which can be cooked directly in the pot.

Safety and Maintenance Tips: Best Practices for Using, Cleaning, and Maintaining Your Crock Pot

Using Your Crock Pot Safely

Never Overfill: Keep the crock pot half to two-thirds full to ensure even cooking.

Keep the Lid On: Lifting the lid during cooking releases heat and can significantly increase cooking time.

Setup: Place your crock pot on a flat, heat-resistant surface away from any walls or cabinets.

Cleaning and Maintenance

Cleaning After Every Use: Allow the crock pot to cool before cleaning. Most removable inserts are dishwasher safe, but always check the manufacturer's recommendations.

Handling the Electronics: Never immerse the base of the crock pot in water. Wipe it down with a damp cloth.

Storage: Store your crock pot with the lid inverted on top of the base, allowing air to circulate and prevent odors.

CHAPTER 2
Tips and Tricks for Crockpot Cooking

Crockpot cooking is all about convenience and bringing out the best in your ingredients. Here are some tips and tricks to help you get the most out of your slow cooker:

1 **Layer Wisely:** Heavier, longer-cooking ingredients like root vegetables and tough cuts of meat should go on the bottom, closer to the heat source. More delicate items, like herbs and dairy, should be added towards the end of cooking to avoid curdling or losing flavor.

2 **Browning is Better:** If you have time, brown your meat in a separate pan before adding it to the crockpot. This extra step adds depth to the flavor through the Maillard reaction, which you don't get from slow cooking alone.

3 **Avoid Overfilling:** To ensure even cooking, fill the crockpot no more than two-thirds full. If it's underfilled, the dish may cook too quickly.

4 **Trim Fat:** Trim excess fat from meats to avoid greasy sauces. Since slow cookers don't allow liquid to evaporate, fat won't render the same way it does in other cooking methods.

5 **Spices and Seasoning:** Some spices can become bitter or lose their flavor over long cooking times. Add delicate herbs and ground spices during the last hour of cooking. Whole herbs and robust spices like bay leaves, cloves, and peppercorns can withstand longer cooking times.

6 **Temperature Control:** Cooking on 'low' generally takes about twice the time as cooking on 'high'. Use the setting that works best for your schedule. If a recipe says 4 hours on high, it'll likely take 8 hours on low.

7 **Don't Peek:** Every time you open the lid, you let out heat and moisture. This can significantly increase the cooking time. Resist the urge to peek until you've reached the final stages of cooking.

8   **Thickening Sauces:** If your sauce is too thin, take the lid off for the last half-hour of cooking, or add a cornstarch slurry (1-2 tablespoons cornstarch mixed with equal parts water) to thicken it up.

9   **Easy Cleanup:** To make cleaning your crockpot a breeze, use a cooking spray or a crockpot liner. This will prevent food from sticking to the sides.

10   **Convert Recipes:** You can convert most oven or stovetop recipes for the crockpot. As a general rule, 1 hour of simmering on the stove or baking at 350 degrees Fahrenheit in the oven equals about 6-8 hours on low or 3-4 hours on high in a crockpot.

11   **Slow Cooker Sizes:** Smaller crockpots (1-3 quarts) are great for dips and side dishes, while larger ones (6-7 quarts) are perfect for roasts and large batches of soup or stew.

12   **Dairy Last:** Milk, cheese, and sour cream should be added during the last 30 minutes of cooking to prevent separation and curdling.

13   **Crispy Finish:** For dishes that benefit from a crispy or broiled top, such as casseroles or mac and cheese, transfer the cooked food to an oven-safe dish and broil it for a few minutes before serving.

14   **Layering for Flavor:** Ingredients like onions and garlic can go in raw, but sautéing them first can add extra flavor to the dish.

15   **Plan Ahead:** Prepare ingredients the night before, keeping them in the fridge. In the morning, you can simply place them into the crockpot, set it, and go about your day.

16   **Less Liquid:** Because slow cookers are sealed, the liquid doesn't evaporate. If you're adapting a standard recipe, reduce the liquid by roughly a third.

(17) Room Temperature: To cook evenly, avoid placing cold ingredients straight from the fridge into the crockpot. Bring them to room temperature first, especially meats, as it allows for more uniform cooking.

(18) Preheating: While not always necessary, preheating your crockpot while you prep your ingredients can save some cooking time.

(19) Distribute Heat: If your slow cooker has a hot spot, place a piece of aluminum foil, folded several times, under the pot to help distribute the heat more evenly.

(20) Acid at the End: Ingredients like wine, lemon juice, or vinegar should be added in the last hour of cooking. Acids can become more pronounced over long cook times, potentially overwhelming your dish.

(21) Cut Uniformly: To ensure even cooking, chop all your vegetables and meat to roughly the same size.

(22) Layer Flavors: Start with a base layer of flavor by using stocks or broths as opposed to water. This adds a depth of flavor to the dish that water alone cannot provide.

(23) Lock in Moisture: If you're cooking something that can dry out, like chicken breast, place it in the liquid to ensure it stays moist.

(24) Utilize the 'Warm' Setting: Many crockpots have a 'warm' setting, which is perfect for keeping food at a safe temperature until you're ready to serve without further cooking it.

(25) Toast Grains: Toast grains like rice or quinoa in a skillet before adding them to the crockpot for an extra layer of nutty flavor.

(26) Sugar and Slow Cooking: Be cautious with sugary ingredients as they can caramelize and potentially burn over the long cooking times. If adding sweet ingredients, do so towards the end of cooking.

(27) Cooking Pasta: If your recipe includes pasta, cook it to just under al dente on the stovetop before adding it to the crockpot. It will continue to cook in the hot liquid of the slow cooker.

(28) Herbs: Fresh herbs can lose flavor over long cooking times. If using fresh, add them towards the end of cooking, or use dried herbs, which hold up better.

(29) Don't Overmix: Avoid stirring too often, especially with casseroles and layered dishes. Crockpots are designed to cook evenly without stirring.

(30) Liquids at the End: If a recipe ends up too liquidy at the end of the cooking time, you can often remove the lid and turn up the heat to high for the last 30 minutes to reduce the liquid.

(31) Making Yogurt: Some advanced slow cookers have settings for fermenting foods like yogurt. It's a low-effort process that can yield delicious results.

(32) Proofing Dough: In colder months, your turned-off crockpot can be a warm spot that's perfect for dough proofing.

(33) Rest Meat: Just like with grilling or roasting, let your meat rest after it comes out of the crockpot before slicing to keep it juicy.

By keeping these additional tips in mind, you can make every crockpot meal a triumph of flavor and texture, and you might just find yourself exploring new culinary territories with this versatile kitchen appliance.

By using these tips and tricks, you'll elevate your crockpot cooking, creating dishes that are both effortless and delectable.

Overnight Oats with Apples and Cinnamon

INGREDIENTS

- 1 cup steel-cut oats
- 4 cups water
- 1 apple, peeled, cored, and chopped
- 1 tsp ground cinnamon
- 2 tbsp honey
- 1/4 tsp salt
- Toppings: chopped nuts, additional honey, or milk (optional)

DIRECTIONS

1. Combine oats, water, apple, cinnamon, honey, and salt in the crockpot.
2. Cook on low for 7-8 hours overnight.
3. Stir before serving and add toppings as desired.

Nutritional Information (per serving, without toppings)

Calories: 150	Fat: 2.5g	Carbohydrates: 27g
Protein: 4g	Sodium: 150mg	Fiber: 4g

Crockpot Egg Casserole

INGREDIENTS

- 12 large eggs
- 1/2 cup milk
- 1 cup shredded cheddar cheese
- 1 small bell pepper, diced
- 1/2 cup diced ham

- 1/2 tsp salt
- 1/4 tsp black pepper
- Cooking spray for the crockpot

DIRECTIONS

1. Whisk together eggs, milk, salt, and pepper.
2. Spray the inside of the crockpot with cooking spray.
3. Layer the ham, bell pepper, and cheese in the crockpot.
4. Pour egg mixture over the layers.
5. Cook on low for 2-3 hours, until eggs are set.

Nutritional Information (per serving):

Calories: 200	Fat: 14g	Carbohydrates: 3g
Protein: 17g	Sodium: 450mg	Fiber: 0.5g

Banana Nut Bread Pudding

INGREDIENTS

- 4 cups cubed whole wheat bread, stale
- 2 ripe bananas, mashed
- 1/3 cup chopped walnuts
- 2 cups milk
- 3 eggs
- 1/4 cup maple syrup
- 1 tsp vanilla extract
- 1/2 tsp cinnamon
- 1/4 tsp nutmeg
- Cooking spray for the crockpot

DIRECTIONS

1. Spray the inside of the crockpot with cooking spray.
2. Place bread cubes in the crockpot.
3. In a bowl, mix together bananas, walnuts, milk, eggs, maple syrup, vanilla, cinnamon, and nutmeg.
4. Pour over the bread, ensuring all pieces are coated.
5. Cook on low for 3-4 hours until the center is set and the edges are slightly browned.

Nutritional Information (per serving)

Calories: 180	Fat: 12g	Carbohydrates: 35g
Protein: 10g	Sodium: 220mg	Fiber: 4g

Crockpot Veggie Omelette

INGREDIENTS

- 8 large eggs
- 1/2 cup milk
- 1 cup fresh spinach, chopped
- 1/2 cup cherry tomatoes, halved
- 1/2 cup feta cheese, crumbled
- 1/4 tsp salt
- 1/4 tsp black pepper
- Cooking spray for the crockpot

DIRECTIONS

1. Whisk together eggs, milk, salt, and pepper.
2. Spray the crockpot with cooking spray.
3. Place spinach, tomatoes, and feta in the crockpot.
4. Pour the egg mixture over the vegetables.
5. Cook on low for 2-3 hours until eggs are set and fully cooked.

Nutritional Information (per serving):

Calories: 170	Fat: 12g	Carbohydrates: 4g
Protein: 13g	Sodium: 400mg	Fiber: 1g

Crockpot French Toast Casserole

INGREDIENTS

- 1 loaf French bread, cut into cubes
- 6 large eggs
- 2 cups milk
- 1/4 cup maple syrup
- 1 tsp vanilla extract
- 1 tsp cinnamon
- 1/4 tsp nutmeg
- Cooking spray for the crockpot

DIRECTIONS

1. Spray the inside of the crockpot with cooking spray and place bread cubes inside.
2. In a bowl, mix eggs, milk, maple syrup, vanilla, cinnamon, and nutmeg.
3. Pour the mixture over the bread, pressing down to
4. soak.
5. Cook on low for 4 hours until puffed and golden.
6. Serve with additional maple syrup if desired.

Nutritional Information (per serving)

Calories: 300	Fat: 8g	Carbohydrates: 44g
Protein: 14g	Sodium: 460mg	Fiber: 2g

Crockpot Berry Breakfast Quinoa

INGREDIENTS

- 1 cup quinoa, rinsed
- 2 cups almond milk
- 2 cups mixed berries (fresh or frozen)
- 2 tbsp honey
- 1 tsp vanilla extract
- 1/2 tsp cinnamon

DIRECTIONS

1. Combine quinoa, almond milk, berries, honey, vanilla, and cinnamon in the crockpot.
2. Cook on low for 6-7 hours or on high for 3-4 hours, until quinoa is cooked through and creamy.
3. Stir well before serving.

Nutritional Information (per serving):

Calories: 220	Fat: 3.5g	Carbohydrates: 40g
Protein: 8g	Sodium: 90mg	Fiber: 5g

Crockpot Southwest Breakfast Burritos

INGREDIENTS

- 1 lb ground turkey breast
- 8 large eggs
- 1/2 cup salsa
- 1/2 cup black beans, drained and rinsed
- 1/2 cup corn
- 1 cup shredded cheddar cheese
- 8 whole wheat tortillas
- Salt and pepper to taste
- Cooking spray for the crockpot

DIRECTIONS

1. Cook ground turkey in a skillet and season with salt and pepper. Transfer to the crockpot.
2. Whisk eggs and salsa together and pour over turkey. Add black beans and corn.
3. Cook on low for 4-5 hours. In the last 30 minutes, sprinkle cheese over the top.
4. Serve on tortillas, rolled into burritos.

Nutritional Information (per serving, 1 burrito)

Calories: 330	Fat: 15g	Carbohydrates: 25g
Protein: 26g	Sodium: 590mg	Fiber: 5g

Crockpot Peaches and Cream Oatmeal

INGREDIENTS

- 2 cups steel-cut oats
- 4 cups water
- 2 cups sliced peaches (fresh or frozen)
- 1 cup cream or non-dairy alternative
- 1/4 cup honey
- 1 tsp vanilla extract
- 1/2 tsp cinnamon
- Pinch of salt

DIRECTIONS

1. Combine oats, water, peaches, cream, honey, vanilla, cinnamon, and salt in the crockpot.
2. Cook on low for 7-8 hours or overnight.
3. Stir well before serving.

Nutritional Information (per serving):

Calories: 310	Fat: 9g	Carbohydrates: 51g
Protein: 8g	Sodium: 80mg	Fiber: 7g

Crockpot Savory Mushroom and Onion Frittata

INGREDIENTS

- 8 large eggs
- 1/2 cup milk
- 1 cup sliced mushrooms
- 1/2 cup diced onion
- 1 cup spinach, chopped
- 1/2 cup grated Parmesan cheese
- Salt and pepper to taste
- Cooking spray for the crockpot

DIRECTIONS

1. Whisk eggs, milk, salt, and pepper.
2. Spray crockpot with cooking spray. Layer mushrooms, onions, spinach, and cheese.
3. Pour the egg mixture over the vegetables.
4. Cook on low for 2-3 hours until the eggs are set.

Nutritional Information (per serving)

Calories: 160	Fat: 10g	Carbohydrates: 4g
Protein: 14g	Sodium: 330mg	Fiber: 1g

Crockpot Apple Butter

INGREDIENTS

- 5 lbs apples, peeled, cored, and sliced
- 1 cup apple cider
- 1/2 cup brown sugar
- 1 tsp ground cinnamon
- 1/4 tsp ground cloves
- 1/4 tsp salt

DIRECTIONS

1. Place all ingredients in the crockpot.
2. Cook on low for 10-12 hours, until the apples are very tender and dark brown.
3. Puree the mixture with an immersion blender or in a standard blender (in batches) until smooth.
4. Serve over toast or with yogurt.

Nutritional Information (per tablespoon):

Calories: 30	Fat: 0g	Carbohydrates: 8g
Protein: 0g	Sodium: 10mg	Fiber: 1g

Slow Cooker Chicken Noodle Soup

INGREDIENTS

- 1 lb boneless, skinless chicken breasts
- 8 cups chicken broth
- 3 carrots, sliced
- 3 celery stalks, sliced
- 1 onion, diced
- 2 cloves garlic, minced
- 1 tsp dried thyme
- 1 tsp dried rosemary
- 1 bay leaf
- Salt and pepper to taste
- 8 oz egg noodles
- Fresh parsley, chopped (for garnish)

DIRECTIONS

1. In the Crockpot, combine chicken breasts, chicken broth, carrots, celery, onion, garlic, dried thyme, dried rosemary, bay leaf, salt, and pepper.
2. Cook on low for 6-8 hours or on high for 3-4 hours, until chicken is cooked through and vegetables are tender.
3. Remove chicken breasts from the Crockpot and shred using two forks. Return shredded chicken to the Crockpot.
4. Add egg noodles to the Crockpot and cook on high for an additional 15-20 minutes, until noodles are tender.
5. Discard the bay leaf. Season with additional salt and pepper if needed.
6. Serve hot, garnished with chopped fresh parsley.

Nutritional Information (per serving)

Calories: 250	Fat: 5g	Carbohydrates: 20g
Protein: 30g	Sodium: 800mg	Fiber: 3g

Crockpot Beef Stew

INGREDIENTS

- 2 lbs beef stew meat, cubed
- 4 cups beef broth
- 1 onion, diced
- 3 carrots, sliced
- 3 potatoes, diced
- 2 cloves garlic, minced
- 2 tbsp tomato paste
- 1 tsp Worcestershire sauce
- 1 tsp dried thyme
- 1 tsp dried rosemary
- Salt and pepper to taste
- 2 tbsp cornstarch (optional, for thickening)
- 2 tbsp water (optional, for cornstarch slurry)
- Fresh parsley, chopped (for garnish)

DIRECTIONS

1. In the Crockpot, combine beef stew meat, beef broth, onion, carrots, potatoes, garlic, tomato paste, Worcestershire sauce, dried thyme, dried rosemary, salt, and pepper.
2. Cook on low for 8-10 hours or on high for 4-6 hours, until beef is tender.
3. If desired, mix cornstarch with water to create a slurry. Stir the slurry into the Crockpot to thicken the stew.
4. Cook on high for an additional 15-30 minutes, until stew is thickened.
5. Serve hot, garnished with chopped fresh parsley.

Nutritional Information (per serving)

Calories: 350	Fat: 10g	Carbohydrates: 25g
Protein: 35g	Sodium: 900mg	Fiber: 4g

Crockpot Lentil Soup

INGREDIENTS

- 1 cup dried green lentils, rinsed and drained
- 6 cups vegetable broth
- 1 onion, diced
- 2 carrots, sliced
- 2 celery stalks, sliced
- 2 cloves garlic, minced

- 1 tsp dried thyme
- 1 tsp dried oregano
- 1 bay leaf
- Salt and pepper to taste
- 2 cups baby spinach
- Lemon wedges (for serving)

DIRECTIONS

1. In the Crockpot, combine dried green lentils, vegetable broth, onion, carrots, celery, garlic, dried thyme, dried oregano, bay leaf, salt, and pepper.
2. Cook on low for 6-8 hours or on high for 3-4 hours, until lentils are tender.
3. Stir in baby spinach and cook for an additional 5-10 minutes, until spinach is wilted.
4. Discard the bay leaf. Season with additional salt and pepper if needed.
5. Serve hot with a squeeze of lemon juice.

Nutritional Information (per serving)

Calories: 200	Fat: 1g	Carbohydrates: 35g
Protein: 15g	Sodium: 800mg	Fiber: 15g

Slow Cooker Chicken Tortilla Soup

INGREDIENTS

- 1 lb boneless, skinless chicken breasts
- 4 cups chicken broth
- 1 onion, diced
- 1 red bell pepper, diced
- 1 can (14.5 oz) diced tomatoes
- 1 can (4 oz) diced green chilies
- 2 cloves garlic, minced
- 1 tsp chili powder
- 1 tsp ground cumin
- Salt and pepper to taste
- Tortilla strips, avocado, shredded cheese, and cilantro (for serving)

DIRECTIONS

1. In the Crockpot, combine chicken breasts, chicken broth, onion, bell pepper, diced tomatoes, diced green chilies, garlic, chili powder, ground cumin, salt, and pepper.
2. Cook on low for 6-8 hours or on high for 3-4 hours, until chicken is cooked through and tender.
3. Remove chicken breasts from the Crockpot and shred using two forks. Return shredded chicken to the Crockpot.
4. Serve hot, garnished with tortilla strips, avocado slices, shredded cheese, and fresh cilantro.

Nutritional Information (per serving)

Calories: 300	Fat: 8g	Carbohydrates: 20g
Protein: 35g	Sodium: 900mg	Fiber: 5g

Crockpot Vegetable Soup

INGREDIENTS

- 6 cups vegetable broth
- 2 carrots, diced
- 2 celery stalks, diced
- 1 onion, diced
- 2 cloves garlic, minced
- 1 can (14.5 oz) diced tomatoes
- 1 cup frozen green beans
- 1 cup frozen corn
- 1 cup frozen peas
- 1 tsp dried thyme
- 1 tsp dried basil
- Salt and pepper to taste
- Fresh parsley, chopped (for garnish)

DIRECTIONS

1. In the Crockpot, combine vegetable broth, carrots, celery, onion, garlic, diced tomatoes (with juices), frozen green beans, frozen corn, frozen peas, dried thyme, dried basil, salt, and pepper.
2. Cook on low for 6-8 hours or on high for 3-4 hours, until vegetables are tender.
3. Season with additional salt and pepper if needed.
4. Serve hot, garnished with chopped fresh parsley.

Nutritional Information (per serving)

Calories: 150	Fat: 1g	Carbohydrates: 30g
Protein: 5g	Sodium: 800mg	Fiber: 8g

Crockpot Butternut Squash Soup

INGREDIENTS

- 1 medium butternut squash, peeled, seeded, and diced
- 1 apple, peeled, cored, and diced
- 1 onion, diced
- 3 cups vegetable broth
- 1 tsp curry powder
- 1/2 tsp ground cinnamon
- 1/4 tsp ground nutmeg
- Salt and pepper to taste
- Coconut milk (for serving)
- Toasted pumpkin seeds (for garnish)

DIRECTIONS

1. In the Crockpot, combine diced butternut squash, diced apple, diced onion, vegetable broth, curry powder, ground cinnamon, ground nutmeg, salt, and pepper.
2. Cook on low for 6-8 hours or on high for 3-4 hours, until squash is tender.
3. Use an immersion blender to puree the soup until smooth.
4. Stir in coconut milk to reach desired creaminess.
5. Serve hot, garnished with toasted pumpkin seeds.

Nutritional Information (per serving)

Calories: 200	Fat: 3g	Carbohydrates: 45g
Protein: 5g	Sodium: 700mg	Fiber: 10g

Slow Cooker Split Pea Soup

INGREDIENTS

- 1 lb dried split peas, rinsed and drained
- 8 cups vegetable broth
- 1 onion, diced
- 2 carrots, diced
- 2 celery stalks, diced
- 2 cloves garlic, minced
- 1 bay leaf
- Salt and pepper to taste
- Croutons (for serving)
- Chopped fresh parsley (for garnish)

DIRECTIONS

1. In the Crockpot, combine dried split peas, vegetable broth, onion, carrots, celery, garlic, bay leaf, salt, and pepper.
2. Cook on low for 8-10 hours or on high for 4-6 hours, until split peas are tender.
3. Discard the bay leaf. Use an immersion blender to puree the soup until smooth.
4. Serve hot, garnished with croutons and chopped fresh parsley.

Nutritional Information (per serving)

Calories: 250	Fat: 1g	Carbohydrates: 45g
Protein: 15g	Sodium: 900mg	Fiber: 20g

Crockpot Potato Soup

INGREDIENTS

- 4 large potatoes, peeled and diced
- 1 onion, diced
- 3 cloves garlic, minced
- 4 cups vegetable broth
- 1 cup milk
- 1/2 cup heavy cream
- 1 cup shredded cheddar cheese
- Salt and pepper to taste
- Chopped chives (for garnish)

DIRECTIONS

1. In the Crockpot, combine diced potatoes, diced onion, minced garlic, vegetable broth, milk, and heavy cream.
2. Cook on low for 6-8 hours or on high for 3-4 hours, until potatoes are tender.
3. Use an immersion blender to blend the soup until smooth.
4. Stir in shredded cheddar cheese until melted.
5. Season with salt and pepper to taste.
6. Serve hot, garnished with chopped chives.

Nutritional Information (per serving)

Calories: 350	Fat: 15g	Carbohydrates: 40g
Protein: 10g	Sodium: 800mg	Fiber: 5g

Crockpot Tomato Basil Soup

INGREDIENTS

- 2 cans (14.5 oz each) diced tomatoes
- 1 onion, diced
- 2 cloves garlic, minced
- 4 cups vegetable broth

- 1/2 cup heavy cream
- 1/4 cup chopped fresh basil
- Salt and pepper to taste
- Grated Parmesan cheese (for serving)

DIRECTIONS

1. In the Crockpot, combine diced tomatoes (with juices), diced onion, minced garlic, and vegetable broth.
2. Cook on low for 6-8 hours or on high for 3-4 hours.
3. Use an immersion blender to blend the soup until smooth.
4. Stir in heavy cream and chopped fresh basil.
5. Season with salt and pepper to taste.
6. Serve hot, garnished with grated Parmesan cheese.

Nutritional Information (per serving)

Calories: 200	Fat: 10g	Carbohydrates: 25g
Protein: 5g	Sodium: 700mg	Fiber: 5g

Slow Cooker Chicken and Rice Soup

INGREDIENTS

- 1 lb boneless, skinless chicken breasts
- 6 cups chicken broth
- 1 onion, diced
- 3 carrots, sliced
- 3 celery stalks, sliced
- 2 cloves garlic, minced
- 1 cup white rice
- 1 tsp dried thyme
- 1 bay leaf
- Salt and pepper to taste
- Chopped fresh parsley (for garnish)

DIRECTIONS

1. In the Crockpot, combine chicken breasts, chicken broth, onion, carrots, celery, garlic, white rice, dried thyme, bay leaf, salt, and pepper.
2. Cook on low for 6-8 hours or on high for 3-4 hours, until chicken is cooked through and rice is tender.
3. Remove chicken breasts from the Crockpot and shred using two forks. Return shredded chicken to the Crockpot.
4. Discard the bay leaf. Season with additional salt and pepper if needed.
5. Serve hot, garnished with chopped fresh parsley.

Nutritional Information (per serving)

Calories: 300	Fat: 5g	Carbohydrates: 30g
Protein: 30g	Sodium: 800mg	Fiber: 3g

Enjoy these hearty and delicious soups and stews made easy with your Crockpot!

Chapter 5: Poultry Recipes

Crockpot BBQ Pulled Chicken

INGREDIENTS

- 2 lbs boneless, skinless chicken breasts
- 1 cup BBQ sauce
- 1/4 cup apple cider vinegar
- 1/4 cup brown sugar
- 1 tbsp Worcestershire sauce
- 1 tsp garlic powder
- 1 tsp onion powder
- Salt and pepper to taste
- Hamburger buns (for serving)

DIRECTIONS

1. In the Crockpot, place the chicken breasts.
2. In a mixing bowl, combine BBQ sauce, apple cider vinegar, brown sugar, Worcestershire sauce, garlic powder, onion powder, salt, and pepper. Pour the mixture over the chicken.
3. Cook on low for 6-8 hours or on high for 3-4 hours, until the chicken is tender and can be easily shredded with a fork.
4. Once cooked, shred the chicken using two forks directly in the Crockpot.
5. Stir the shredded chicken in the sauce until evenly coated.
6. Serve the BBQ pulled chicken on hamburger buns.

Nutritional Information (per serving, without bun)

Calories: 250	Fat: 3g	Carbohydrates: 20g
Protein: 30g	Sodium: 600mg	Fiber: 1g

Enjoy these hearty and delicious soups and stews made easy with your Crockpot!

Crockpot Lemon Garlic Chicken

INGREDIENTS

- 2 lbs boneless, skinless chicken thighs
- 1/4 cup lemon juice
- 1/4 cup chicken broth
- 2 tbsp olive oil
- 4 cloves garlic, minced
- 1 tsp dried thyme
- 1 tsp dried rosemary
- Salt and pepper to taste
- Fresh parsley, chopped (for garnish)

DIRECTIONS

1. In the Crockpot, place the chicken thighs.
2. In a mixing bowl, combine lemon juice, chicken broth, olive oil, minced garlic, dried thyme, dried rosemary, salt, and pepper. Pour the mixture over the chicken.
3. Cook on low for 6-8 hours or on high for 3-4 hours, until the chicken is cooked through and tender.
4. Once cooked, sprinkle chopped fresh parsley over the chicken before serving.

Nutritional Information (per serving)

Calories: 280	Fat: 14g	Carbohydrates: 2g
Protein: 35g	Sodium: 400mg	Fiber: 0g

Crockpot Chicken Tikka Masala

INGREDIENTS

- 2 lbs boneless, skinless chicken breasts, cut into bite-sized pieces
- 1 onion, finely chopped
- 3 cloves garlic, minced
- 1 tbsp ginger, minced
- 1 cup tomato sauce
- 1 cup plain yogurt
- 2 tbsp olive oil
- 2 tbsp garam masala
- 1 tsp ground cumin
- 1 tsp paprika
- 1/2 tsp ground cinnamon
- Salt and pepper to taste
- Cooked rice (for serving)
- Chopped fresh cilantro (for garnish)

DIRECTIONS

1. In the Crockpot, place the chicken pieces, chopped onion, minced garlic, and minced ginger.
2. In a mixing bowl, combine tomato sauce, plain yogurt, olive oil, garam masala, ground cumin, paprika, ground cinnamon, salt, and pepper. Pour the mixture over the chicken.
3. Stir to coat the chicken evenly with the sauce.
4. Cook on low for 6-8 hours or on high for 3-4 hours, until the chicken is cooked through and tender.
5. Serve the chicken tikka masala over cooked rice, garnished with chopped fresh cilantro.

Nutritional Information (per serving, without rice)

Calories: 320	Fat: 14g	Carbohydrates: 9g
Protein: 38g	Sodium: 600mg	Fiber: 2g

Crockpot Honey Garlic Chicken

INGREDIENTS

- 2 lbs boneless, skinless chicken thighs
- 1/2 cup honey
- 1/4 cup soy sauce
- 2 tbsp ketchup
- 2 cloves garlic, minced
- 1 tbsp olive oil
- 1 tsp dried basil
- 1/2 tsp dried oregano
- Salt and pepper to taste
- Sesame seeds (for garnish)
- Sliced green onions (for garnish)

DIRECTIONS

1. In the Crockpot, place the chicken thighs.
2. In a mixing bowl, combine honey, soy sauce, ketchup, minced garlic, olive oil, dried basil, dried oregano, salt, and pepper. Pour the mixture over the chicken.
3. Cook on low for 6-8 hours or on high for 3-4 hours, until the chicken is cooked through and tender.
4. Once cooked, sprinkle sesame seeds and sliced green onions over the chicken before serving.

Nutritional Information (per serving)

Calories: 290	Fat: 9g	Carbohydrates: 22g
Protein: 30g	Sodium: 700mg	Fiber: 0g

Crockpot Chicken Enchilada Casserole

INGREDIENTS

- 2 lbs boneless, skinless chicken breasts
- 1 onion, diced
- 1 red bell pepper, diced
- 1 can (15 oz) black beans, drained and rinsed
- 1 can (15 oz) corn kernels, drained
- 1 can (10 oz) red enchilada sauce
- 1 cup shredded cheddar cheese
- 1 cup shredded Monterey Jack cheese
- 1 tbsp chili powder
- 1 tsp ground cumin
- Salt and pepper to taste
- Tortilla chips (for serving)
- Sour cream (for serving)
- Sliced jalapenos (for garnish)
- Chopped fresh cilantro (for garnish)

DIRECTIONS

1. In the Crockpot, place the chicken breasts, diced onion, diced red bell pepper, black beans, and corn kernels.
2. In a mixing bowl, combine red enchilada sauce, shredded cheddar cheese, shredded Monterey Jack cheese, chili powder, ground cumin, salt, and pepper. Pour the mixture over the chicken and vegetables.
3. Cook on low for 6-8 hours or on high for 3-4 hours, until the chicken is cooked through and tender.
4. Once cooked, shred the chicken using two forks and stir to combine with the sauce and vegetables.
5. Serve the chicken enchilada casserole over tortilla chips, garnished with sour cream, sliced jalapenos, and chopped fresh cilantro.

Nutritional Information (per serving, without tortilla chips and toppings)

Calories: 350	Fat: 15g	Carbohydrates: 25g
Protein: 30g	Sodium: 800mg	Fiber: 5g

Crockpot Chicken Alfredo

INGREDIENTS

- 2 lbs boneless, skinless chicken thighs
- 2 cups chicken broth
- 1 cup heavy cream
- 1/2 cup grated Parmesan cheese
- 4 cloves garlic, minced
- 1 tsp dried basil
- 1/2 tsp dried thyme
- Salt and pepper to taste
- 16 oz fettuccine pasta, cooked according to package instructions
- Chopped fresh parsley (for garnish)

DIRECTIONS

1. In the Crockpot, place the chicken thighs.
2. In a mixing bowl, combine chicken broth, heavy cream, grated Parmesan cheese, minced garlic, dried basil, dried thyme, salt, and pepper. Pour the mixture over the chicken.
3. Cook on low for 6-8 hours or on high for 3-4 hours, until the chicken is cooked through and tender.
4. Once cooked, remove the chicken from the Crockpot and shred using two forks. Return shredded chicken to the Crockpot.
5. Stir to combine the shredded chicken with the sauce.
6. Serve the chicken Alfredo over cooked fettuccine pasta, garnished with chopped fresh parsley.

Nutritional Information (per serving, without pasta)

Calories: 320	Fat: 20g	Carbohydrates: 6g
Protein: 30g	Sodium: 500mg	Fiber: 0g

Slow Cooker Spicy Buffalo Chicken Melt

INGREDIENTS

- 2 lbs boneless, skinless chicken breasts
- 1 block (8 oz) cream cheese, softened
- 1 cup buffalo sauce
- 1 cup shredded cheddar cheese
- 1/2 cup ranch dressing
- 1/4 cup chopped green onions
- Tortilla chips or celery sticks (for serving)

DIRECTIONS

1. In the Crockpot, place the chicken breasts.
2. In a mixing bowl, combine softened cream cheese, buffalo sauce, shredded cheddar cheese, ranch dressing, and chopped green onions. Pour the mixture over the chicken.
3. Cook on low for 6-8 hours or on high for 3-4 hours, until the chicken is cooked through and tender.
4. Once cooked, shred the chicken using two forks and stir to combine with the sauce.
5. Serve the buffalo chicken dip warm, with tortilla chips or celery sticks for dipping.

Nutritional Information (per serving, without chips or celery sticks)

Calories: 280

Fat: 15g

Carbohydrates: 4g

Protein: 30g

Sodium: 800mg

Fiber: 0g

Crockpot Teriyaki Chicken Wings

INGREDIENTS

- 2 lbs chicken wings
- 1/2 cup soy sauce
- 1/4 cup honey
- 2 cloves garlic, minced
- 1 tsp grated ginger
- 1 tbsp cornstarch
- 1 tbsp water
- Sesame seeds (for garnish)
- Sliced green onions (for garnish)

DIRECTIONS

1. In the Crockpot, place the chicken wings.
2. In a mixing bowl, combine soy sauce, honey, minced garlic, and grated ginger. Pour the mixture over the chicken wings.
3. Cook on low for 6-8 hours or on high for 3-4 hours, until the chicken wings are cooked through and tender.
4. Once cooked, remove the chicken wings from the Crockpot and place them on a baking sheet.
5. In a small bowl, mix cornstarch and water to make a slurry. Stir the slurry into the sauce in the Crockpot to thicken.
6. Brush the thickened sauce over the chicken wings.
7. Broil the chicken wings in the oven for 5-7 minutes, until caramelized and crispy.
8. Serve the teriyaki chicken wings hot, garnished with sesame seeds and sliced green onions.

Nutritional Information (per serving, without pasta)

Calories: 280	Fat: 15g	Carbohydrates: 15g
Protein: 20g	Sodium: 900mg	Fiber: 0g

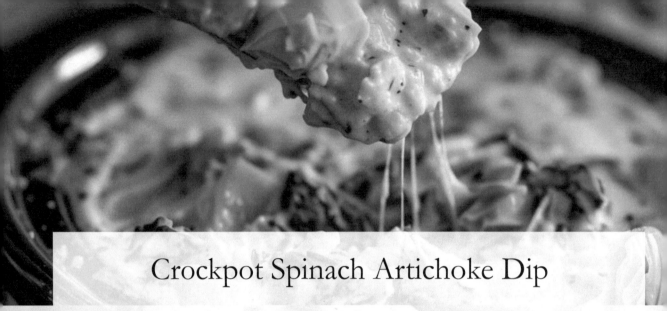

Crockpot Spinach Artichoke Dip

INGREDIENTS

- 2 cups frozen spinach, thawed and drained
- 1 can (14 oz) artichoke hearts, drained and chopped
- 1 block (8 oz) cream cheese, softened
- 1/2 cup sour cream
- 1/2 cup mayonnaise
- 1 cup shredded mozzarella cheese
- 1/2 cup grated Parmesan cheese
- 2 cloves garlic, minced
- 1/2 tsp onion powder
- 1/2 tsp garlic powder
- Salt and pepper to taste
- Tortilla chips or bread slices (for serving)

DIRECTIONS

1. In the Crockpot, combine thawed and drained spinach, chopped artichoke hearts, softened cream cheese, sour cream, mayonnaise, shredded mozzarella cheese, grated Parmesan cheese, minced garlic, onion powder, garlic powder, salt, and pepper.
2. Stir until well combined.
3. Cook on low for 2-3 hours or on high for 1-2 hours, until the dip is hot and bubbly.
4. Stir the dip occasionally while cooking.
5. Once cooked, serve the spinach artichoke dip hot, with tortilla chips or bread slices for dipping.

Nutritional Information (per serving, without chips or bread)

Calories: 280	Fat: 25g	Carbohydrates: 5g
Protein: 10g	Sodium: 600mg	Fiber: 2g

Crockpot Buffalo Chicken Meatballs

INGREDIENTS

- 1 lb ground chicken
- 1/4 cup breadcrumbs
- 1/4 cup buffalo sauce
- 1 egg
- 1/2 tsp garlic powder
- 1/2 tsp onion powder
- Salt and pepper to taste
- 1/2 cup buffalo sauce (for sauce)
- 2 tbsp unsalted butter (for sauce)
- Sliced green onions (for garnish)
- Crumbled blue cheese (for garnish)
- Toothpicks (for serving)

DIRECTIONS

1. In a mixing bowl, combine ground chicken, breadcrumbs, buffalo sauce, egg, garlic powder, onion powder, salt, and pepper. Mix until well combined.
2. Shape the mixture into small meatballs.
3. In the Crockpot, place the meatballs.
4. In a small saucepan, combine buffalo sauce and unsalted butter. Heat over medium heat until the butter is melted and the sauce is heated through.
5. Pour the buffalo sauce mixture over the meatballs in the Crockpot.
6. Cook on low for 2-3 hours or on high for 1-2 hours, until the meatballs are cooked through.
7. Once cooked, serve the buffalo chicken meatballs hot, garnished with sliced green onions and crumbled blue cheese, with toothpicks for serving.

Nutritional Information (per serving, without garnishes)

Calories: 200	Fat: 12g	Carbohydrates: 5g
Protein: 18g	Sodium: 600mg	Fiber: 0.5g

Chapter 6: Beef & Pork Recipes

Slow Cooker BBQ Pulled Pork

INGREDIENTS

- 3 lbs pork shoulder or butt
- 1 cup BBQ sauce
- 1/2 cup apple cider vinegar
- 1/4 cup brown sugar
- 1 tbsp Worcestershire sauce
- 1 tbsp chili powder
- 1 tsp garlic powder
- 1 tsp onion powder
- Salt and pepper to taste

DIRECTIONS

1. Place the pork shoulder or butt in the Crockpot.
2. In a mixing bowl, combine BBQ sauce, apple cider vinegar, brown sugar, Worcestershire sauce, chili powder, garlic powder, onion powder, salt, and pepper. Pour the mixture over the pork.
3. Cook on low for 8-10 hours or on high for 4-6 hours, until the pork is tender and easily shreds with a fork.
4. Once cooked, shred the pork using two forks and mix it with the sauce.
5. Serve the pulled pork on buns or rolls, topped with additional BBQ sauce if desired.

Nutritional Information (per serving)

Calories: 350	Fat: 18g	Carbohydrates: 20g
Protein: 25g	Sodium: 700mg	Fiber: 1g

Savory Slow Cooker Beef Stew

INGREDIENTS

- 2 lbs beef stew meat, cubed
- 4 cups beef broth
- 1 cup red wine (optional)
- 2 carrots, peeled and chopped
- 2 potatoes, peeled and chopped
- 1 onion, diced
- 2 cloves garlic, minced
- 2 tbsp tomato paste
- 1 tsp dried thyme
- 1 tsp dried rosemary
- Salt and pepper to taste

DIRECTIONS

1. Place the beef stew meat in the Crockpot.
2. Add beef broth, red wine (if using), carrots, potatoes, onion, garlic, tomato paste, dried thyme, dried rosemary, salt, and pepper to the Crockpot.
3. Stir to combine.
4. Cook on low for 8-10 hours or on high for 4-6 hours, until the beef and vegetables are tender.
5. Once cooked, adjust seasoning if needed and serve the beef stew hot.

Nutritional Information (per serving)

Calories: 320	Fat: 12g	Carbohydrates: 20g
Protein: 30g	Sodium: 800mg	Fiber: 3g

Slow Cooker Beef Chili

INGREDIENTS

- 2 lbs ground beef
- 1 onion, diced
- 3 cloves garlic, minced
- 2 cans (14.5 oz each) diced tomatoes
- 1 can (15 oz) kidney beans, drained and rinsed
- 1 can (15 oz) black beans, drained and rinsed
- 1 cup beef broth
- 2 tbsp chili powder
- 1 tbsp cumin
- 1 tsp paprika
- Salt and pepper to taste

DIRECTIONS

1. In a skillet, cook ground beef over medium heat until browned. Drain excess fat.
2. Transfer the cooked beef to the Crockpot.
3. Add diced onion, minced garlic, diced tomatoes, kidney beans, black beans, beef broth, chili powder, cumin, paprika, salt, and pepper to the Crockpot.
4. Stir to combine.
5. Cook on low for 6-8 hours or on high for 3-4 hours, until the flavors meld together.
6. Once cooked, adjust seasoning if needed and serve the beef chili hot, topped with optional toppings like shredded cheese, sour cream, or chopped green onions.

Nutritional Information (per serving)

Calories: 380	Fat: 18g	Carbohydrates: 25g
Protein: 30g	Sodium: 900mg	Fiber: 8g

Crockpot Beef and Broccoli

INGREDIENTS

- 2 lbs beef sirloin, thinly sliced
- 1 cup beef broth
- 1/2 cup soy sauce
- 1/4 cup brown sugar
- 3 cloves garlic, minced
- 2 tbsp cornstarch
- 2 tbsp water
- 4 cups broccoli florets
- Cooked rice (for serving)

DIRECTIONS

1. Place the thinly sliced beef sirloin in the Crockpot.
2. In a mixing bowl, combine beef broth, soy sauce, brown sugar, and minced garlic. Pour the mixture over the beef.
3. Cook on low for 4-6 hours or on high for 2-3 hours, until the beef is cooked through and tender.
4. In a small bowl, mix cornstarch and water to make a slurry. Stir the slurry into the sauce in the Crockpot to thicken.
5. Add broccoli florets to the Crockpot during the last 30 minutes of cooking.
6. Once cooked, serve the beef and broccoli over cooked rice.

Nutritional Information (per serving, without rice)

Calories: 280	Fat: 10g	Carbohydrates: 15g
Protein: 30g	Sodium: 800mg	Fiber: 3g

Crockpot Beef Tacos

INGREDIENTS

- 2 lbs beef chuck roast
- 1 onion, diced
- 1 can (4 oz) diced green chilies
- 1 can (14.5 oz) diced tomatoes
- 2 tbsp chili powder
- 1 tbsp cumin
- 1 tsp paprika
- Salt and pepper to taste
- Corn or flour tortillas (for serving)
- **Optional toppings:** shredded lettuce, diced tomatoes, shredded cheese, salsa, sour cream

DIRECTIONS

1. Place the beef chuck roast in the Crockpot.
2. Add diced onion, diced green chilies, diced tomatoes, chili powder, cumin, paprika, salt, and pepper to the Crockpot.
3. Cook on low for 8-10 hours or on high for 4-6 hours, until the beef is fork-tender and shreds easily.
4. Once cooked, shred the beef using two forks and mix it with the sauce.
5. Serve the beef filling in corn or flour tortillas, topped with optional toppings like shredded lettuce, diced tomatoes, shredded cheese, salsa, and sour cream.

Nutritional Information (per serving, without tortillas or toppings)

Calories: 320	Fat: 15g	Carbohydrates: 10g
Protein: 30g	Sodium: 700mg	Fiber: 2g

Slow Cooker Beef and Mushroom Stroganoff

INGREDIENTS

- 2 lbs beef stew meat, cubed
- 1 onion, diced
- 2 cloves garlic, minced
- 8 oz mushrooms, sliced
- 2 cups beef broth
- 1 cup sour cream
- 2 tbsp Worcestershire sauce
- 1 tbsp Dijon mustard
- 2 tbsp cornstarch
- 2 tbsp water
- Cooked egg noodles (for serving)

DIRECTIONS

1. Place the beef stew meat, diced onion, minced garlic, and sliced mushrooms in the Crockpot.
2. In a mixing bowl, whisk together beef broth, sour cream, Worcestershire sauce, and Dijon mustard. Pour the mixture over the beef and mushrooms.
3. Cook on low for 6-8 hours or on high for 3-4 hours, until the beef is tender.
4. In a small bowl, mix cornstarch and water to make a slurry. Stir the slurry into the sauce in the Crockpot to thicken.
5. Once cooked, serve the beef and mushroom stroganoff over cooked egg noodles.

Nutritional Information (per serving, without noodles)

Calories: 350	Fat: 18g	Carbohydrates: 10g
Protein: 30g	Sodium: 700mg	Fiber: 1g

Crockpot Beef Bourguignon

INGREDIENTS

- 2 lbs beef chuck roast, cut into chunks
- 1 onion, diced
- 2 carrots, peeled and sliced
- 2 stalks celery, sliced
- 8 oz mushrooms, quartered
- 2 cups beef broth
- 1 cup red wine (optional)
- 2 tbsp tomato paste
- 2 cloves garlic, minced
- 2 tbsp all-purpose flour
- Salt and pepper to taste
- Chopped fresh parsley (for garnish)

DIRECTIONS

1. Place the beef chuck roast chunks, diced onion, sliced carrots, sliced celery, quartered mushrooms, beef broth, red wine (if using), tomato paste, minced garlic, all-purpose flour, salt, and pepper in the Crockpot.
2. Stir to combine.
3. Cook on low for 8-10 hours or on high for 4-6 hours, until the beef is tender.
4. Once cooked, adjust seasoning if needed and serve the beef bourguignon hot, garnished with chopped fresh parsley.

Nutritional Information (per serving)

Calories: 380	Fat: 15g	Carbohydrates: 15g
Protein: 35g	Sodium: 800mg	Fiber: 3g

Slow Cooker Korean Beef

INGREDIENTS

- 2 lbs beef chuck roast, thinly sliced
- 1 onion, thinly sliced
- 4 cloves garlic, minced
- 1/2 cup soy sauce
- 1/4 cup brown sugar
- 2 tbsp rice vinegar
- 1 tbsp sesame oil
- 1 tbsp ginger, grated
- 1 tsp red pepper flakes
- 2 green onions, sliced (for garnish)
- Cooked rice (for serving)
- Sesame seeds (for garnish)

DIRECTIONS

1. Place the thinly sliced beef chuck roast, thinly sliced onion, minced garlic, soy sauce, brown sugar, rice vinegar, sesame oil, grated ginger, and red pepper flakes in the Crockpot.
2. Stir to combine.
3. Cook on low for 6-8 hours or on high for 3-4 hours, until the beef is tender.
4. Once cooked, serve the Korean beef over cooked rice, garnished with sliced green onions and sesame seeds.

Nutritional Information (per serving, without rice)

Calories: 320	Fat: 15g	Carbohydrates: 15g
Protein: 30g	Sodium: 800mg	Fiber: 1g

Crockpot Beef Barbacoa

INGREDIENTS

- 2 lbs beef chuck roast
- 1 onion, diced
- 4 cloves garlic, minced
- 1 chipotle pepper in adobo sauce, chopped
- 1 tbsp adobo sauce (from the chipotle pepper can)
- 1/4 cup lime juice

- 2 tsp ground cumin
- 2 tsp dried oregano
- 1 tsp ground cloves
- Salt and pepper to taste
- Chopped fresh cilantro (for garnish)
- Lime wedges (for serving)
- Corn or flour tortillas (for serving)

DIRECTIONS

1. Place the beef chuck roast, diced onion, minced garlic, chopped chipotle pepper, adobo sauce, lime juice, ground cumin, dried oregano, ground cloves, salt, and pepper in the Crockpot.
2. Stir to combine.
3. Cook on low for 8-10 hours or on high for 4-6 hours, until the beef is tender.
4. Once cooked, shred the beef using two forks and mix it with the sauce.
5. Serve the beef barbacoa in corn or flour tortillas, garnished with chopped fresh cilantro and lime wedges.

Nutritional Information (per serving, without tortillas)

Calories: 320	Fat: 15g	Carbohydrates: 10g
Protein: 30g	Sodium: 700mg	Fiber: 1g

Slow Cooker Beef Ragu

INGREDIENTS

- 2 lbs beef chuck roast
- 1 onion, diced
- 2 carrots, peeled and diced
- 2 stalks celery, diced
- 4 cloves garlic, minced
- 1 can (28 oz) crushed tomatoes
- 1 cup beef broth
- 1/2 cup red wine (optional)
- 2 tbsp tomato paste
- 2 tsp dried oregano
- 2 tsp dried basil
- Salt and pepper to taste
- Cooked pasta (for serving)
- Grated Parmesan cheese (for serving)
- Chopped fresh parsley (for garnish)

DIRECTIONS

1. Place the beef chuck roast, diced onion, diced carrots, diced celery, minced garlic, crushed tomatoes, beef broth, red wine (if using), tomato paste, dried oregano, dried basil, salt, and pepper in the Crockpot.
2. Stir to combine.
3. Cook on low for 8-10 hours or on high for 4-6 hours, until the beef is tender and falls apart easily.
4. Once cooked, shred the beef using two forks and mix it with the sauce.
5. Serve the beef ragu over cooked pasta, garnished with grated Parmesan cheese and chopped fresh parsley.

Nutritional Information (per serving, without pasta and toppings)

Calories: 350	Fat: 18g	Carbohydrates: 10g
Protein: 35g	Sodium: 800mg	Fiber: 2g

Crockpot New England Clam Chowder

INGREDIENTS

- 2 lbs clams, scrubbed and cleaned
- 4 slices bacon, diced
- 1 onion, diced
- 2 stalks celery, diced
- 2 carrots, peeled and diced
- 3 cups diced potatoes
- 4 cups seafood or vegetable broth
- 1 cup heavy cream
- 2 tbsp all-purpose flour
- Salt and pepper to taste
- Chopped fresh parsley (for garnish)

DIRECTIONS

1. Place the cleaned clams, diced bacon, diced onion, diced celery, diced carrots, diced potatoes, and seafood or vegetable broth in the Crockpot.
2. Stir to combine.
3. Cook on low for 4-6 hours or on high for 2-3 hours, until the vegetables are tender and the clams have opened.
4. Once cooked, remove the clams from the shells, chop them, and return them to the Crockpot.
5. In a small bowl, whisk together heavy cream and all-purpose flour until smooth. Stir the mixture into the chowder to thicken.
6. Season with salt and pepper to taste.
7. Serve the clam chowder hot, garnished with chopped fresh parsley.

Nutritional Information (per serving)

Calories: 280	Fat: 12g	Carbohydrates: 30g
Protein: 15g	Sodium: 700mg	Fiber: 3g

Slow Cooker Shrimp Scampi

INGREDIENTS

- 1 lb large shrimp, peeled and deveined
- 4 cloves garlic, minced
- 1/4 cup white wine (optional)
- 1/4 cup chicken broth
- 2 tbsp lemon juice
- 2 tbsp unsalted butter
- 2 tbsp chopped fresh parsley
- Salt and pepper to taste
- Cooked pasta (for serving)
- Grated Parmesan cheese (for serving)

DIRECTIONS

1. Place the peeled and deveined shrimp, minced garlic, white wine (if using), chicken broth, lemon juice, unsalted butter, chopped fresh parsley, salt, and pepper in the Crockpot.
2. Stir to combine.
3. Cook on low for 1-2 hours or on high for 30-45 minutes, until the shrimp are pink and cooked through.
4. Once cooked, serve the shrimp scampi over cooked pasta, garnished with grated Parmesan cheese.

Nutritional Information (per serving, without pasta and cheese)

Calories: 200	Fat: 8g	Carbohydrates: 4g
Protein: 25g	Sodium: 600mg	Fiber: 1g

Crockpot Seafood Gumbo

INGREDIENTS

- 1 lb shrimp, peeled and deveined
- 1 lb crab meat
- 1 lb smoked sausage, sliced
- 1 onion, diced
- 1 bell pepper, diced
- 2 stalks celery, diced
- 4 cloves garlic, minced
- 1 can (14.5 oz) diced tomatoes
- 4 cups seafood or chicken broth
- 1/4 cup all-purpose flour
- 1/4 cup unsalted butter
- 2 tbsp Cajun seasoning
- Cooked rice (for serving)
- Chopped fresh parsley (for garnish)

DIRECTIONS

1. Place the peeled and deveined shrimp, crab meat, sliced smoked sausage, diced onion, diced bell pepper, diced celery, minced garlic, diced tomatoes, seafood or chicken broth, and Cajun seasoning in the Crockpot.
2. Stir to combine.
3. Cook on low for 6-8 hours or on high for 3-4 hours, until the flavors meld together.
4. In a small saucepan, melt unsalted butter over medium heat. Whisk in all-purpose flour to make a roux. Cook, stirring constantly, until the roux turns golden brown.
5. Stir the roux into the gumbo in the Crockpot to thicken.
6. Once cooked, serve the seafood gumbo over cooked rice, garnished with chopped fresh parsley.

Nutritional Information (per serving, without rice)

Calories: 320	Fat: 18g	Carbohydrates: 10g
Protein: 30g	Sodium: 900mg	Fiber: 2g

Slow Cooker Crab Dip

INGREDIENTS

- 1 lb lump crab meat
- 8 oz cream cheese, softened
- 1/2 cup mayonnaise
- 1/4 cup sour cream
- 1/4 cup grated Parmesan cheese
- 2 cloves garlic, minced
- 1/4 tsp Old Bay seasoning
- Salt and pepper to taste
- Chopped fresh chives (for garnish)
- Tortilla chips or crackers (for serving)

DIRECTIONS

1. Place the lump crab meat, softened cream cheese, mayonnaise, sour cream, grated Parmesan cheese, minced garlic, Old Bay seasoning, salt, and pepper in the Crockpot.
2. Stir to combine.
3. Cook on low for 1-2 hours or on high for 30-45 minutes, until the dip is hot and bubbly.
4. Once cooked, stir the dip to combine all ingredients evenly.
5. Serve the crab dip hot, garnished with chopped fresh chives, alongside tortilla chips or crackers.

Nutritional Information (per serving, without chips or crackers)

Calories: 180	Fat: 15g	Carbohydrates: 2g
Protein: 10g	Sodium: 400mg	Fiber: 0g

Crockpot Lemon Garlic Butter Scallops

INGREDIENTS

- 1 lb scallops
- 4 cloves garlic, minced
- 1/4 cup unsalted butter, melted
- 2 tbsp lemon juice
- 1 tbsp chopped fresh parsley
- Salt and pepper to taste
- Cooked rice or pasta (for serving)

DIRECTIONS

1. Place the scallops, minced garlic, melted unsalted butter, lemon juice, chopped fresh parsley, salt, and pepper in the Crockpot.
2. Stir to combine.
3. Cook on low for 1-2 hours or on high for 30-45 minutes, until the scallops are opaque and cooked through.
4. Once cooked, serve the lemon garlic butter scallops over cooked rice or pasta.

Nutritional Information (per serving, without rice or pasta)

Calories: 180

Fat: 10g

Carbohydrates: 4g

Protein: 18g

Sodium: 450mg

Fiber: 0g

Slow Cooker Cajun Shrimp and Sausage

INGREDIENTS

- 1 lb shrimp, peeled and deveined
- 1 lb smoked sausage, sliced
- 1 onion, diced
- 1 bell pepper, diced
- 2 stalks celery, diced
- 4 cloves garlic, minced
- 1 can (14.5 oz) diced tomatoes
- 1 cup chicken broth
- 2 tbsp Cajun seasoning
- Cooked rice (for serving)
- Chopped fresh parsley (for garnish)

DIRECTIONS

1. Place the peeled and deveined shrimp, sliced smoked sausage, diced onion, diced bell pepper, diced celery, minced garlic, diced tomatoes, chicken broth, and Cajun seasoning in the Crockpot.
2. Stir to combine.
3. Cook on low for 4-6 hours or on high for 2-3 hours, until the flavors meld together.
4. Once cooked, serve the Cajun shrimp and sausage over cooked rice, garnished with chopped fresh parsley.

Nutritional Information (per serving, without rice)

Calories: 280

Fat: 15g

Carbohydrates: 10g

Protein: 25g

Sodium: 900mg

Fiber: 2g

Crockpot Garlic Butter Mussels

INGREDIENTS

- 2 lbs mussels, cleaned and debearded
- 4 cloves garlic, minced
- 1/4 cup unsalted butter, melted
- 1/4 cup white wine
- 2 tbsp chopped fresh parsley
- Salt and pepper to taste
- Crusty bread (for serving)

DIRECTIONS

1. Place the cleaned and debearded mussels, minced garlic, melted unsalted butter, white wine, chopped fresh parsley, salt, and pepper in the Crockpot.
2. Stir to combine.
3. Cook on low for 1-2 hours or on high for 30-45 minutes, until the mussels have opened.
4. Once cooked, serve the garlic butter mussels hot, with crusty bread for dipping.

Nutritional Information (per serving, without bread)

Calories: 200

Fat: 12g

Carbohydrates: 5g

Protein: 15g

Sodium: 600mg

Fiber: 0g

Slow Cooker Coconut Curry Shrimp

INGREDIENTS

- 1 lb shrimp, peeled and deveined
- 1 onion, diced
- 2 cloves garlic, minced
- 1 bell pepper, diced
- 1 carrot, peeled and sliced
- 1 can (14 oz) coconut milk
- 2 tbsp red curry paste
- 1 tbsp fish sauce
- 1 tbsp brown sugar
- 1 tbsp lime juice
- Cooked rice (for serving)
- Chopped fresh cilantro (for garnish)

DIRECTIONS

1. Place the peeled and deveined shrimp, diced onion, minced garlic, diced bell pepper, sliced carrot, coconut milk, red curry paste, fish sauce, brown sugar, and lime juice in the Crockpot.
2. Stir to combine.
3. Cook on low for 2-3 hours or on high for 1-2 hours, until the shrimp are pink and cooked through.
4. Once cooked, serve the coconut curry shrimp over cooked rice, garnished with chopped fresh cilantro.

Nutritional Information (per serving, without rice)

Calories: 250

Fat: 15g

Carbohydrates: 10g

Protein: 20g

Sodium: 800mg

Fiber: 2g

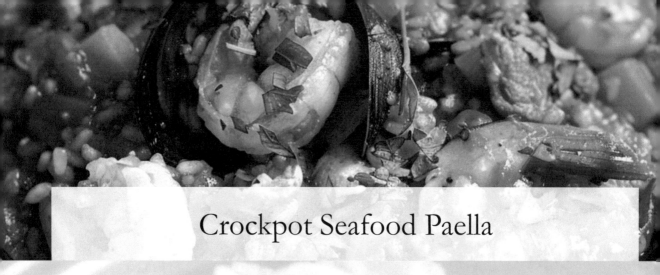

Crockpot Seafood Paella

INGREDIENTS

- 1 lb shrimp, peeled and deveined
- 1 lb mussels, cleaned and debearded
- 1 lb clams, scrubbed and cleaned
- 1 onion, diced
- 2 bell peppers, diced
- 4 cloves garlic, minced
- 1 can (14.5 oz) diced tomatoes
- 2 cups chicken broth
- 1 1/2 cups Arborio rice
- 1/2 cup frozen peas
- 1/2 tsp saffron threads
- Salt and pepper to taste
- Chopped fresh parsley (for garnish)
- Lemon wedges (for serving)

DIRECTIONS

1. Place the peeled and deveined shrimp, cleaned and debearded mussels, scrubbed and cleaned clams, diced onion, diced bell peppers, minced garlic, diced tomatoes, chicken broth, Arborio rice, frozen peas, saffron threads, salt, and pepper in the Crockpot.
2. Stir to combine.
3. Cook on low for 3-4 hours or on high for 1-2 hours, until the seafood is cooked through and the rice is tender.
4. Once cooked, serve the seafood paella hot, garnished with chopped fresh parsley and lemon wedges.

Nutritional Information (per serving)

Calories: 350	Fat: 10g	Carbohydrates: 40g
Protein: 25g	Sodium: 900mg	Fiber: 3g

Slow Cooker Seafood Cioppino

INGREDIENTS

- 1 lb shrimp, peeled and deveined
- 1 lb mussels, cleaned and debearded
- 1 lb clams, scrubbed and cleaned
- 1 onion, diced
- 4 cloves garlic, minced
- 1 bell pepper, diced
- 2 stalks celery, diced
- 1 can (14.5 oz) diced tomatoes
- 1 cup seafood or chicken broth
- 1/2 cup dry white wine
- 2 tbsp tomato paste
- 1 tbsp Italian seasoning
- Salt and pepper to taste
- Chopped fresh parsley (for garnish)
- Crusty bread (for serving)

DIRECTIONS

1. Place the peeled and deveined shrimp, cleaned and debearded mussels, scrubbed and cleaned clams, diced onion, minced garlic, diced bell pepper, diced celery, diced tomatoes, seafood or chicken broth, dry white wine, tomato paste, Italian seasoning, salt, and pepper in the Crockpot.
2. Stir to combine.
3. Cook on low for 4-6 hours or on high for 2-3 hours, until the seafood is cooked through and the flavors meld together.
4. Once cooked, serve the seafood cioppino hot, garnished with chopped fresh parsley, and with crusty bread for dipping.

Nutritional Information (per serving, without bread)

Calories: 300	Fat: 8g	Carbohydrates: 20g
Protein: 30g	Sodium: 900mg	Fiber: 3g

Enjoy these delicious slow cooker seafood recipes, perfect for convenient and flavorful meals!

Chapter 8: Vegetarian Recipes

Slow Cooker Lentil Soup

INGREDIENTS

- 1 cup dried green lentils
- 4 cups vegetable broth
- 1 onion, diced
- 2 carrots, diced
- 2 celery stalks, diced
- 2 cloves garlic, minced
- 1 can (14.5 oz) diced tomatoes
- 1 tsp dried thyme
- 1 tsp dried oregano
- Salt and pepper to taste
- Fresh parsley, chopped (for garnish)

DIRECTIONS

1. Rinse the dried green lentils under cold water and drain.
2. In the crockpot, combine the rinsed lentils, vegetable broth, diced onion, diced carrots, diced celery, minced garlic, diced tomatoes (with their juices), dried thyme, dried oregano, salt, and pepper.
3. Stir to combine all ingredients.
4. Cook on low for 6-8 hours or on high for 3-4 hours, until the lentils and vegetables are tender.
5. Once cooked, taste and adjust seasoning if needed.
6. Serve the lentil soup hot, garnished with chopped fresh parsley.

Nutritional Information (per serving)

Calories: 180	Fat: 1g	Carbohydrates: 32g
Protein: 12g	Sodium: 600mg	Fiber: 14g

Crockpot Vegetarian Chili

INGREDIENTS

- 1 can (15 oz) kidney beans, drained and rinsed
- 1 can (15 oz) black beans, drained and rinsed
- 1 can (15 oz) pinto beans, drained and rinsed
- 1 can (14.5 oz) diced tomatoes
- 1 onion, diced
- 2 bell peppers, diced

- 2 cloves garlic, minced
- 1 cup frozen corn kernels
- 1 cup vegetable broth
- 2 tbsp chili powder
- 1 tsp ground cumin
- Salt and pepper to taste
- **Optional toppings:** shredded cheese, diced avocado, chopped cilantro, sour cream

DIRECTIONS

1. In the crockpot, combine the drained and rinsed kidney beans, black beans, pinto beans, diced tomatoes (with their juices), diced onion, diced bell peppers, minced garlic, frozen corn kernels, vegetable broth, chili powder, ground cumin, salt, and pepper.
2. Stir to combine all ingredients.
3. Cook on low for 6-8 hours or on high for 3-4 hours, until the flavors meld together and the chili thickens.
4. Once cooked, taste and adjust seasoning if needed.
5. Serve the vegetarian chili hot, topped with shredded cheese, diced avocado, chopped cilantro, and sour cream if desired.

Nutritional Information (per serving, without toppings)

Calories: 250	Fat: 1g	Carbohydrates: 50g
Protein: 15g	Sodium: 800mg	Fiber: 15g

Slow Cooker Vegetable Curry

INGREDIENTS

- 1 can (15 oz) chickpeas, drained and rinsed
- 2 cups cauliflower florets
- 2 cups sweet potato, diced
- 1 onion, diced
- 2 cloves garlic, minced
- 1 can (14 oz) coconut milk
- 1 can (14.5 oz) diced tomatoes
- 2 tbsp curry powder
- 1 tsp ground turmeric
- 1 tsp ground ginger
- Salt and pepper to taste
- Cooked rice or naan bread (for serving)

DIRECTIONS

1. In the crockpot, combine the drained and rinsed chickpeas, cauliflower florets, diced sweet potato, diced onion, minced garlic, coconut milk, diced tomatoes (with their juices), curry powder, ground turmeric, ground ginger, salt, and pepper.
2. Stir to combine all ingredients.
3. Cook on low for 6-8 hours or on high for 3-4 hours, until the vegetables are tender and the curry thickens.
4. Once cooked, taste and adjust seasoning if needed.
5. Serve the vegetable curry hot, over cooked rice or with naan bread on the side.

Nutritional Information (per serving, without rice or naan)

Calories: 280	Fat: 10g	Carbohydrates: 40g
Protein: 10g	Sodium: 700mg	Fiber: 10g

Slow-Simmered Golden Squash Soup

INGREDIENTS

- 1 medium butternut squash, peeled, seeded, and diced
- 1 apple, peeled, cored, and diced
- 1 onion, diced
- 2 cloves garlic, minced
- 4 cups vegetable broth

- 1 tsp ground cinnamon
- 1/2 tsp ground nutmeg
- Salt and pepper to taste
- **Optional toppings:** roasted pumpkin seeds, Greek yogurt, chopped fresh parsley

DIRECTIONS

1. In the crockpot, combine the diced butternut squash, diced apple, diced onion, minced garlic, vegetable broth, ground cinnamon, ground nutmeg, salt, and pepper.
2. Stir to combine all ingredients.
3. Cook on low for 6-8 hours or on high for 3-4 hours, until the butternut squash is tender.
4. Once cooked, use an immersion blender to blend the soup until smooth. Alternatively, transfer the soup in batches to a blender and blend until smooth, then return to the crockpot.
5. Taste and adjust seasoning if needed.
6. Serve the butternut squash soup hot, topped with roasted pumpkin seeds, a dollop of Greek yogurt, and chopped fresh parsley if desired.

Nutritional Information (per serving, without toppings)		
Calories: 150	Fat: 1g	Carbohydrates: 35g
Protein: 3g	Sodium: 600mg	Fiber: 8g

Slow Cooker Ratatouille

INGREDIENTS

- 1 eggplant, diced
- 2 zucchini, diced
- 1 yellow squash, diced
- 1 onion, diced
- 2 bell peppers, diced
- 4 cloves garlic, minced
- 1 can (14.5 oz) diced tomatoes
- 2 tbsp tomato paste
- 1 tsp dried basil
- 1 tsp dried oregano
- Salt and pepper to taste
- Fresh basil leaves, chopped (for garnish)

DIRECTIONS

1. In the crockpot, combine the diced eggplant, diced zucchini, diced yellow squash, diced onion, diced bell peppers, minced garlic, diced tomatoes (with their juices), tomato paste, dried basil, dried oregano, salt, and pepper.
2. Stir to combine all ingredients.
3. Cook on low for 6-8 hours or on high for 3-4 hours, until the vegetables are tender.
4. Once cooked, taste and adjust seasoning if needed.
5. Serve the ratatouille hot, garnished with chopped fresh basil leaves.

Nutritional Information (per serving)

Calories: 120	Fat: 1g	Carbohydrates: 25g
Protein: 5g	Sodium: 600mg	Fiber: 8g

Crockpot Quinoa and Black Bean Stuffed Peppers

INGREDIENTS

- 4 bell peppers, halved and seeds removed
- 1 cup quinoa, rinsed
- 1 can (15 oz) black beans, drained and rinsed
- 1 can (14.5 oz) diced tomatoes
- 1 onion, diced
- 2 cloves garlic, minced
- 1 tsp chili powder
- 1 tsp ground cumin
- Salt and pepper to taste
- Shredded cheese (for topping)
- Chopped cilantro (for garnish)

DIRECTIONS

1. In the crockpot, place the halved bell peppers.
2. In a bowl, combine the rinsed quinoa, drained and rinsed black beans, diced tomatoes (with their juices), diced onion, minced garlic, chili powder, ground cumin, salt, and pepper.
3. Stir to combine all ingredients.
4. Spoon the quinoa and black bean mixture into each bell pepper half.
5. Cover the crockpot and cook on low for 4-6 hours or on high for 2-3 hours, until the peppers are tender.
6. Once cooked, sprinkle shredded cheese over each stuffed pepper and let it melt.
7. Serve the quinoa and black bean stuffed peppers hot, garnished with chopped cilantro.

Nutritional Information (per serving, one pepper half)

Calories: 200	Fat: 3g	Carbohydrates: 35g
Protein: 10g	Sodium: 600mg	Fiber: 8g

Slow Cooker Mushroom Risotto

INGREDIENTS

- 2 cups Arborio rice
- 4 cups vegetable broth
- 1 onion, diced
- 2 cloves garlic, minced
- 8 oz mushrooms, sliced
- 1/2 cup dry white wine
- 1/4 cup grated Parmesan cheese
- Salt and pepper to taste
- Chopped fresh parsley (for garnish)

DIRECTIONS

1. In the crockpot, combine the Arborio rice, vegetable broth, diced onion, minced garlic, sliced mushrooms, dry white wine, salt, and pepper.
2. Stir to combine all ingredients.
3. Cover the crockpot and cook on low for 2-3 hours, until the rice is tender and creamy.
4. Once cooked, stir in the grated Parmesan cheese until melted and well combined.
5. Taste and adjust seasoning if needed.
6. Serve the mushroom risotto hot, garnished with chopped fresh parsley.

Nutritional Information (per serving)

Calories: 250	Fat: 2g	Carbohydrates: 50g
Protein: 8g	Sodium: 800mg	Fiber: 3g

Crockpot Vegetable Lasagna

INGREDIENTS

- 9 lasagna noodles, uncooked
- 3 cups marinara sauce
- 2 cups ricotta cheese
- 2 cups shredded mozzarella cheese
- 1 zucchini, thinly sliced
- 1 yellow squash, thinly sliced
- 1 bell pepper, thinly sliced
- 1 onion, thinly sliced
- 2 cloves garlic, minced
- Salt and pepper to taste
- Chopped fresh basil (for garnish)

DIRECTIONS

1. In a bowl, mix together the marinara sauce and minced garlic.
2. Spread a thin layer of the marinara sauce mixture on the bottom of the crockpot.
3. Place 3 lasagna noodles over the sauce, breaking them if needed to fit.
4. Spread half of the ricotta cheese over the noodles, followed by half of the sliced zucchini, yellow squash, bell pepper, and onion.
5. Sprinkle half of the shredded mozzarella cheese over the vegetables.
6. Repeat the layers with the remaining ingredients, ending with a layer of shredded mozzarella cheese on top.
7. Cover the crockpot and cook on low for 4-6 hours or on high for 2-3 hours, until the noodles are tender and the cheese is melted and bubbly.
8. Once cooked, let the vegetable lasagna rest for a few minutes before slicing.
9. Serve the vegetable lasagna hot, garnished with chopped fresh basil.

Nutritional Information (per serving)

Calories: 350	Fat: 12g	Carbohydrates: 40g
Protein: 20g	Sodium: 700mg	Fiber: 5g

Slow Cooker Sweet Potato and Black Bean Enchiladas

INGREDIENTS

- 2 sweet potatoes, peeled and diced
- 1 can (15 oz) black beans, drained and rinsed
- 1 onion, diced
- 2 cloves garlic, minced
- 1 bell pepper, diced
- 1 cup frozen corn kernels
- 1 can (14.5 oz) diced tomatoes
- 1 cup enchilada sauce
- 2 cups shredded Mexican cheese blend, divided
- 8 corn tortillas
- Salt and pepper to taste
- Chopped fresh cilantro (for garnish)

DIRECTIONS

1. In the crockpot, combine the diced sweet potatoes, drained and rinsed black beans, diced onion, minced garlic, diced bell pepper, frozen corn kernels, diced tomatoes (with their juices), enchilada sauce, 1 cup shredded Mexican cheese blend, salt, and pepper.
2. Stir to combine all ingredients.
3. Spoon a thin layer of the sweet potato and black bean mixture onto the bottom of the crockpot.
4. Place 2 corn tortillas over the mixture, overlapping if needed.
5. Repeat the layers with the remaining ingredients, ending with a layer of the sweet potato and black bean mixture on top.
6. Sprinkle the remaining shredded Mexican cheese blend over the top.
7. Cover the crockpot and cook on low for 4-6 hours or on high for 2-3 hours, until the enchiladas are heated through and the cheese is melted and bubbly.

8. Once cooked, let the enchiladas rest for a few minutes before serving.
9. Serve the sweet potato and black bean enchiladas hot, garnished with chopped fresh cilantro.

Nutritional Information (per serving)

Calories: 300	Fat: 8g	Carbohydrates: 45g
Protein: 15g	Sodium: 800mg	Fiber: 8g

Crockpot Cauliflower Tikka Masala

INGREDIENTS

- 1 head cauliflower, cut into florets
- 1 onion, diced
- 3 cloves garlic, minced
- 1 can (14 oz) coconut milk
- 1 can (14.5 oz) diced tomatoes
- 2 tbsp tomato paste
- 2 tbsp garam masala
- 1 tsp ground turmeric
- 1 tsp ground ginger
- Salt and pepper to taste
- Cooked rice or naan bread (for serving)
- Chopped fresh cilantro (for garnish)

DIRECTIONS

1. In the crockpot, combine the cauliflower florets, diced onion, minced garlic, coconut milk, diced tomatoes (with their juices), tomato paste, garam masala, ground turmeric, ground ginger, salt, and pepper.
2. Stir to combine all ingredients.
3. Cook on low for 6-8 hours or on high for 3-4 hours, until the cauliflower is tender and the flavors meld together.
4. Once cooked, taste and adjust seasoning if needed.
5. Serve the cauliflower tikka masala hot, over cooked rice or with naan bread on the side, garnished with chopped fresh cilantro.

Nutritional Information (per serving, without rice or naan)

Calories: 180

Fat: 10g

Carbohydrates: 20g

Protein: 5g

Sodium: 600mg

Fiber: 5g

Chapter 9: Deserts Recipes

Crockpot Apple Crisp

INGREDIENTS

- 6 cups sliced apples (about 6 medium-sized apples)
- 1/2 cup granulated sugar
- 1 teaspoon ground cinnamon
- 1/4 teaspoon ground nutmeg
- 1 cup old-fashioned oats
- 1/2 cup all-purpose flour
- 1/2 cup packed brown sugar
- 1/2 cup unsalted butter, melted

DIRECTIONS

1. In a large bowl, toss the sliced apples with granulated sugar, ground cinnamon, and ground nutmeg until evenly coated.
2. Transfer the seasoned apples to the crockpot.
3. In the same bowl, mix together the old-fashioned oats, all-purpose flour, brown sugar, and melted butter until crumbly.
4. Sprinkle the oat mixture evenly over the apples in the crockpot.
5. Cover and cook on low for 4-6 hours or on high for 2-3 hours, until the apples are tender and the topping is golden brown and crispy.
6. Serve the apple crisp warm, optionally with a scoop of vanilla ice cream.

Nutritional Information (per serving)

Calories: 250	Fat: 8g	Carbohydrates: 45g
Protein: 2g	Sodium: 10mg	Fiber: 5g

Slow Cooker Chocolate Lava Cake

INGREDIENTS

- 1 cup all-purpose flour
- 1/2 cup granulated sugar
- 1/4 cup unsweetened cocoa powder
- 1 1/2 teaspoons baking powder
- 1/4 teaspoon salt
- 1/2 cup milk
- 1/4 cup unsalted butter, melted
- 1 teaspoon vanilla extract
- 1/2 cup semisweet chocolate chips
- 3/4 cup packed brown sugar
- 1 1/2 cups hot water

DIRECTIONS

1. In a mixing bowl, whisk together the all-purpose flour, granulated sugar, cocoa powder, baking powder, and salt.
2. Stir in the milk, melted butter, and vanilla extract until smooth.
3. Fold in the semisweet chocolate chips.
4. Spread the batter evenly in the bottom of the crockpot.
5. In a separate bowl, mix together the packed brown sugar and hot water until dissolved.
6. Pour the brown sugar mixture over the batter in the crockpot.
7. Cover and cook on high for 2-3 hours, until the cake is set around the edges but still gooey in the center.
8. Serve the chocolate lava cake warm, optionally with whipped cream or vanilla ice cream.

Nutritional Information (per serving)

Calories: 300	Fat: 10g	Carbohydrates: 55g
Protein: 4g	Sodium: 150mg	Fiber: 3g

Slow Cooker Berry Cobbler

INGREDIENTS

- 4 cups mixed berries (such as strawberries, blueberries, raspberries)
- 1/4 cup granulated sugar
- 1 tablespoon lemon juice
- 1 cup all-purpose flour
- 1/2 cup granulated sugar
- 1 teaspoon baking powder
- 1/4 teaspoon salt
- 1/2 cup unsalted butter, melted
- Vanilla ice cream (for serving)

DIRECTIONS

1. In the crockpot, combine the mixed berries, granulated sugar, and lemon juice. Toss until the berries are evenly coated.
2. In a separate bowl, mix together the all-purpose flour, granulated sugar, baking powder, and salt.
3. Stir in the melted butter until a crumbly dough forms.
4. Sprinkle the dough evenly over the berries in the crockpot.
5. Cover and cook on low for 3-4 hours or on high for 2-3 hours, until the berries are bubbly and the topping is golden brown.
6. Serve the berry cobbler warm, topped with vanilla ice cream.

Nutritional Information (per serving)

Calories: 300	Fat: 10g	Carbohydrates: 50g
Protein: 3g	Sodium: 150mg	Fiber: 5g

Slow Cooker Banana Bread Pudding

INGREDIENTS

- 4 ripe bananas, mashed
- 2 cups of whole wheat bread, cubed (ensure it's a day old for best texture)
- 1/2 cup of walnuts, chopped (optional for added omega-3 fatty acids)
- 3 eggs, beaten
- 1 1/2 cups unsweetened almond milk
- 1 teaspoon pure vanilla extract
- 1/3 cup maple syrup
- 1/2 teaspoon ground cinnamon
- 1/4 teaspoon ground nutmeg
- 1/4 teaspoon salt

DIRECTIONS

1. **Prepare the Slow Cooker:** Grease the inside of your slow cooker pot with a little olive oil or use a cooking spray to prevent sticking.
2. **Combine Bananas and Bread:** In the slow cooker, mix together the mashed bananas and cubed bread. Add the chopped walnuts if using.
3. **Mix Wet Ingredients:** In a separate bowl, whisk together the beaten eggs, unsweetened almond milk, vanilla extract, maple syrup, cinnamon, nutmeg, and salt.
4. **Combine Everything:** Pour the egg mixture over the bread and bananas in the slow cooker. Gently stir to ensure all the bread is soaked evenly.
5. **Cook:** Cover the slow cooker and set it to cook on low for about 4 hours, or until the pudding is set and the edges begin to pull away from the sides of the cooker.
6. **Serve:** Serve warm directly from the slow cooker. Optional to garnish with additional cinnamon or a drizzle of extra maple syrup.

Nutritional Information (per serving, based on 6 servings)

Calories: 280	Fat: 8g	Carbohydrates: 46g
Protein: 8g	Sodium: 220mg	Fiber: 6g

Slow Cooker Bread Pudding with Bourbon Sauce

INGREDIENTS

For Bread Pudding:
- 6 cups cubed French bread
- 4 large eggs
- 2 cups whole milk
- 1/2 cup granulated sugar
- 1 teaspoon vanilla extract
- 1/2 teaspoon ground cinnamon
- 1/4 teaspoon ground nutmeg
- 1/2 cup raisins (optional)

For Bourbon Sauce:
- 1/2 cup unsalted butter
- 1 cup packed brown sugar
- 1/4 cup heavy cream
- 2 tablespoons bourbon (optional)

DIRECTIONS

1. In the crockpot, combine the cubed French bread, eggs, milk, granulated sugar, vanilla extract, ground cinnamon, ground nutmeg, and raisins (if using). Stir until well combined.
2. Cover and cook on low for 3-4 hours, until the bread pudding is set and golden brown on top.
3. Meanwhile, prepare the bourbon sauce. In a saucepan, melt the butter over medium heat. Stir in the brown sugar and heavy cream until smooth. Bring to a simmer and cook for 2-3 minutes, stirring constantly.
4. Remove the saucepan from heat and stir in the bourbon (if using).
5. Serve the bread pudding warm, drizzled with bourbon sauce.

Nutritional Information (per serving, bread pudding only)

Calories: 320	Fat: 12g	Carbohydrates: 48g
Protein: 6g	Sodium: 200mg	Fiber: 2g

Nutritional Information (per serving, bourbon sauce only)

Calories: 120	Fat: 8g	Carbohydrates: 15g
Protein: 0g	Sodium: 20mg	Fiber: 0g

Slow Cooker Chocolate Fondue

INGREDIENTS

- 1 cup heavy cream
- 2 cups semisweet chocolate chips
- 1 teaspoon vanilla extract

- Assorted dipping ingredients (such as strawberries, banana slices, marshmallows, and pretzels)

DIRECTIONS

1. In the crockpot, combine the heavy cream, semisweet chocolate chips, and vanilla extract.
2. Cover and cook on low for 1-2 hours, stirring occasionally, until the chocolate is melted and smooth.
3. Once melted, reduce the crockpot heat to warm to keep the fondue warm and smooth.
4. Serve the chocolate fondue with assorted dipping ingredients for a delicious dessert experience.

Nutritional Information (per serving, chocolate fondue only)

Calories: 200   Fat: 15g   Carbohydrates: 15g

Protein: 2g   Sodium: 20mg   Fiber: 2g

Crockpot Bread Pudding

INGREDIENTS

- 6 cups cubed bread (such as French bread or brioche)
- 4 large eggs
- 2 cups milk
- 1/2 cup granulated sugar
- 1 teaspoon vanilla extract
- 1/2 teaspoon ground cinnamon
- 1/4 teaspoon ground nutmeg
- 1/2 cup raisins (optional)
- 1/4 cup unsalted butter, melted

DIRECTIONS

1. Place the cubed bread in the crockpot.
2. In a mixing bowl, whisk together the eggs, milk, granulated sugar, vanilla extract, ground cinnamon, and ground nutmeg until well combined.
3. Pour the egg mixture over the bread in the crockpot.
4. Sprinkle the raisins (if using) evenly over the top.
5. Drizzle the melted butter over the top.
6. Gently press down on the bread to ensure it's fully submerged in the egg mixture.
7. Cover and cook on low for 3-4 hours, until the bread pudding is set and golden brown on top.
8. Serve the bread pudding warm, optionally with a dusting of powdered sugar or a drizzle of caramel sauce.

Nutritional Information (per serving)

Calories: 300	Fat: 10g	Carbohydrates: 45g
Protein: 8g	Sodium: 250mg	Fiber: 2g

Slow Cooker Rice Pudding

INGREDIENTS

- 1 cup long-grain white rice
- 4 cups milk
- 1/2 cup granulated sugar
- 1 teaspoon vanilla extract
- 1/4 teaspoon ground cinnamon
- 1/4 teaspoon salt
- 1/2 cup raisins (optional)
- Ground nutmeg (for garnish)

DIRECTIONS

1. Rinse the long-grain white rice under cold water until the water runs clear.
2. In the crockpot, combine the rinsed rice, milk, granulated sugar, vanilla extract, ground cinnamon, and salt.
3. Stir until well combined.
4. Cover and cook on low for 2-3 hours, stirring occasionally, until the rice is tender and the mixture has thickened.
5. Stir in the raisins (if using) during the last 30 minutes of cooking.
6. Once cooked, spoon the rice pudding into serving bowls.
7. Sprinkle ground nutmeg over the top for garnish.
8. Serve the rice pudding warm or chilled.

Nutritional Information (per serving)

Calories: 250	Fat: 5g	Carbohydrates: 45g
Protein: 6g	Sodium: 200mg	Fiber: 1g

Crockpot Peach Cobbler

INGREDIENTS

- 4 cups sliced peaches (fresh or canned)
- 1/4 cup granulated sugar
- 1 tablespoon lemon juice
- 1 cup all-purpose flour
- 1/2 cup granulated sugar
- 1 teaspoon baking powder
- 1/4 teaspoon salt
- 1/2 cup unsalted butter, melted
- Vanilla ice cream (for serving)

DIRECTIONS

1. In a bowl, toss the sliced peaches with granulated sugar and lemon juice until well coated.
2. Transfer the peaches to the crockpot.
3. In a separate bowl, mix together the all-purpose flour, granulated sugar, baking powder, and salt.
4. Stir in the melted butter until a crumbly dough forms.
5. Sprinkle the dough evenly over the peaches in the crockpot.
6. Cover and cook on low for 3-4 hours or on high for 2-3 hours, until the cobbler is bubbly and the topping is golden brown.
7. Serve the peach cobbler warm, topped with vanilla ice cream.

Nutritional Information (per serving)

Calories: 300   Fat: 10g   Carbohydrates: 50g

Protein: 3g   Sodium: 150mg   Fiber: 3g

Slow Cooker Creamy Vanilla Bean Risotto

INGREDIENTS

- 1 cup Arborio rice
- 3 cups unsweetened almond milk
- 1 cup light coconut milk
- 1 vanilla bean, split lengthwise, or
- 1 teaspoon pure vanilla extract

- 1/4 cup maple syrup
- A pinch of sea salt
- **Optional toppings:** Fresh berries (like blueberries or raspberries) or a sprinkle of ground cinnamon

DIRECTIONS

1. **Prepare Ingredients:** If using a vanilla bean, split it lengthwise and scrape out the seeds.
2. **Combine in Cooker:** In the slow cooker, combine the Arborio rice, unsweetened almond milk, light coconut milk, and the vanilla bean seeds or extract. Add a pinch of sea salt.
3. **Cook:** Cover and set the slow cooker to low. Cook for about 3-4 hours, stirring occasionally until the rice is tender and the mixture has a creamy consistency. Depending on your slow cooker, you may need to adjust the cooking time slightly.
4. **Final Touch:** Once the risotto is done, remove the vanilla bean pod (if used) and stir in the maple syrup. Mix well to ensure everything is evenly sweetened and flavored.
5. **Serve:** Spoon the risotto into bowls. Serve warm, topped with fresh berries and a sprinkle of cinnamon, if desired.

Nutritional Information (per serving, based on 6 servings, without toppings)

Calories: 230	Fat: 4g	Carbohydrates: 42g
Protein: 4g	Sodium: 80mg	Fiber: 2g

CHAPTER 10
28-Day Meal Plan

Overview

This 30-day meal plan is designed to reduce the stress of meal planning while ensuring that each dish is both nourishing and satisfying. Each week includes breakfasts, lunches, dinners, and a few delightful snacks or desserts, all tailored to maximize the use of your crock pot.

Weekly Breakdown

Each week is structured to provide a balanced diet with recipes that are both diverse and appealing, ensuring that you never tire of the same flavors.

WEEK 1: INTRODUCTION TO SLOW COOKING

Days	Breakfast	Lunch	Dinner	Dessert
Day 1	Overnight Oats with Apples and Cinnamon (Page# 14)	Crockpot Buffalo Chicken Meatballs (Page# 43)	Crockpot BBQ Pulled Chicken (Page# 34)	Crockpot Apple Crisp (Page# 75)
Day 2	Crockpot Egg Casserole (Page# 15)	Crockpot Beef Stew (Page# 25)	Slow Cooker BBQ Pulled Pork (Page# 44)	
Day 3	Banana Nut Bread Pudding (Page# 16)	Crockpot Lentil Soup (Page# 26)	Crockpot Lemon Garlic Chicken (Page# 35)	
Day 4	Crockpot Veggie Omelette (Page# 17)	Slow Cooker Chicken Tortilla Soup (Page# 27)	Crockpot Beef and Broccoli (Page# 47)	
Day 5	Crockpot French Toast Casserole (Page# 18)	Crockpot Vegetable Soup (Page# 28)	Crockpot Honey Garlic Chicken (Page# 37)	Slow Cooker Chocolate Fondue (Page# 80)
Day 6	Crockpot Berry Breakfast Quinoa (Page# 19)	Crockpot Butternut Squash Soup (Page# 29)	Crockpot Beef Tacos (Page# 48)	
Day 7	Crockpot Southwest Breakfast Burritos (Page# 20)	Slow Cooker Split Pea Soup (Page# 30)	Crockpot Chicken Enchilada Casserole (Page# 38)	

WEEK 2: EXPLORING GLOBAL CUISINES

Days	Breakfast	Lunch	Dinner	Dessert
Day 8	Crockpot Peaches and Cream Oatmeal (Page# 21)	Crockpot Potato Soup (Page# 31)	Crockpot Chicken Alfredo (Page# 39)	
Day 9	Crockpot Savory Mushroom and Onion Frittata (Page# 22)	Crockpot Tomato Basil Soup (Page# 32)	Slow Cooker Beef and Mushroom Stroganoff (Page# 49)	
Day 10	Crockpot Apple Butter (Page# 23)	Slow Cooker Chicken and Rice Soup (Page# 33)	Slow Cooker Spicy Buffalo Chicken Melt (Page# 40)	Slow Cooker Banana Bread Pudding (Page# 78)
Day 11	Overnight Oats with Apples and Cinnamon (Page# 14)	Crockpot Vegetarian Chili (Page# 65)	Crockpot Beef Bourguignon (Page# 50)	
Day 12	Crockpot Egg Casserole (Page# 15)	Slow Cooker Vegetable Curry (Page# 66)	Slow Cooker Korean Beef (Page# 51)	
Day 13	Banana Nut Bread Pudding (Page# 16)	Slow-Simmered Golden Squash Soup (Page# 67)	Crockpot Teriyaki Chicken Wings (Page# 41)	
Day 14	Crockpot Veggie Omelette (Page# 17)	Slow Cooker Ratatouille (Page# 68)	Crockpot Spinach Artichoke Dip (Page# 42)	Slow Cooker Bread Pudding with Bourbon Sauce (Page# 79)

WEEK 3: COMFORT FOODS

Days	Breakfast	Lunch	Dinner	Dessert
Day 15	Crockpot French Toast Casserole (Page# 18)	Crockpot Quinoa and Black Bean Stuffed Peppers (Page# 69)	Slow Cooker Beef Chili (Page# 46)	
Day 16	Crockpot Berry Breakfast Quinoa (Page# 19)	Slow Cooker Mushroom Risotto (Page# 70)	Crockpot Beef Barbacoa (Page# 52)	Crockpot Bread Pudding (Page# 81)
Day 17	Crockpot Southwest Breakfast Burritos (Page# 20)	Crockpot Vegetable Lasagna (Page# 71)	Slow Cooker Crab Dip (Page# 57)	
Day 18	Crockpot Peaches and Cream Oatmeal (Page# 21)	Slow Cooker Sweet Potato and Black Bean Enchiladas (Page# 72)	Crockpot New England Clam Chowder (Page# 54)	
Day 19	Crockpot Savory Mushroom and Onion Frittata (Page# 22)	Crockpot Cauliflower Tikka Masala (Page# 74)	Slow Cooker Shrimp Scampi (Page# 55)	
Day 20	Crockpot Apple Butter (Page# 23)	Crockpot Lentil Soup (Page# 26)	Crockpot Seafood Gumbo (Page# 56)	Slow Cooker Rice Pudding (Page# 82)
Day 21	Overnight Oats with Apples and Cinnamon (Page# 14)	Crockpot Vegetarian Chili (Page# 65)	Crockpot Lemon Garlic Butter Scallops (Page# 58)	

WEEK 4: KEEPING IT LIGHT

Days	Breakfast	Lunch	Dinner	Dessert
Day 22	Crockpot Egg Casserole (Page# 15)	Slow Cooker Vegetable Curry (Page# 66)	Slow Cooker Cajun Shrimp and Sausage (Page# 59)	
Day 23	Banana Nut Bread Pudding (Page# 16)	Slow-Simmered Golden Squash Soup (Page# 67)	Crockpot Garlic Butter Mussels (Page# 60)	
Day 24	Crockpot Veggie Omelette (Page# 17)	Slow Cooker Ratatouille (Page# 68)	Slow Cooker Coconut Curry Shrimp (Page# 61)	
Day 25	Crockpot French Toast Casserole (Page# 18)	Crockpot Quinoa and Black Bean Stuffed Peppers (Page# 69)	Crockpot Seafood Paella (Page# 62)	Crockpot Peach Cobbler (Page# 83)
Day 26	Crockpot Berry Breakfast Quinoa (Page# 19)	Slow Cooker Mushroom Risotto (Page# 70)	Slow Cooker Seafood Cioppino (Page# 63)	
Day 27	Crockpot Southwest Breakfast Burritos (Page# 20)	Crockpot Vegetable Lasagna (Page# 71)	Crockpot Beef and Broccoli (Page# 47)	
Day 28	Crockpot Peaches and Cream Oatmeal (Page# 21)	Slow Cooker Sweet Potato and Black Bean Enchiladas (Page# 72)	Slow Cooker Berry Cobbler (Page# 77)	Slow Cooker Creamy Vanilla Bean Risotto (Page# 84)

How to Use a 28-Day Meal Plan

1. **Review the Plan in Advance:**
   Before you start, familiarize yourself with the entire meal plan. Understand the variety of meals and snacks included and make sure you have all the necessary information about portion sizes and preparation methods.

2. **Customize When Necessary:**
   Adjust the meal plan to fit your specific dietary needs and preferences. Swap out any ingredients or meals that don't suit you or that you know may affect your blood glucose negatively. Always ensure that the substitutions align with your nutritional goals.

3. **Prepare Weekly Shopping Lists:**
   Divide your meal plan into weekly segments and prepare shopping lists for each week. Stick to the list to avoid impulsive purchases that are not part of your diet plan. This also helps in managing food budget and waste.

4. **Batch Cook and Prep:**
   Take advantage of days when you have more time to cook meals in batches. Preparing multiple meals in advance can save time during busier days and ensures that you stick to your meal plan.

5. **Monitor Your Blood Sugar Levels:**
   Keep a close track of your blood sugar levels as you follow the meal plan. This will help you identify the foods that work best for you and any adjustments that need to be made to the meal plan.

6. **Stay Hydrated and Consider Timing:**
   Make sure to drink plenty of water throughout the day. Also, pay attention to the timing of your meals and snacks to maintain a steady level of blood sugar throughout the day.

7. **Seek Support:**
   Share your meal plan with family or friends who can provide encouragement and support. If possible, involve them in meal preparation to make cooking more enjoyable and less of a chore. Using a structured 28-day meal plan can help you make significant strides in managing diabetes through diet. By planning ahead and preparing properly, you can enjoy a diverse range of foods and maintain your health effortlessly.

Conclusion

As we come to the end of this culinary journey through the slow simmering world of Crockpot cooking, it's important to reflect on what we've discovered together. This cookbook is more than a collection of recipes—it's an invitation to embrace the art of slow cooking, which transforms simple ingredients into exquisite meals that comfort, delight, and satisfy.

Each page of this book has offered you not just a recipe, but a doorway into the flavors and aromas that only time can cultivate. From robust chilis that warm chilly evenings to tender roasts that gather the family around the table, each dish has been a testament to the patience required in slow cooking—and the rewards it yields.

But beyond the delicious meals, this journey has also been about rediscovering the joy of cooking without haste. In today's fast-paced world, taking the time to cook slowly may seem like a luxury, but it's a profoundly fulfilling one. A slow cooker allows you to step back and let the flavors do the hard work, giving you back your time to focus on what truly matters: sharing these meals with loved ones.

As you continue to explore these recipes and make them your own, remember that each ingredient added to your Crockpot carries with it the promise of a meal that will offer comfort and joy to those who gather at your table. Here's to the adventures that await in your culinary future, to the simplicity and depth of slow-cooked meals, and to the delicious satisfaction that comes from knowing you've fed your loved ones well.

Thank you for allowing this cookbook to be a part of your kitchen. May your slow cooker be always bubbling with something wonderful, and may your home be filled with the fragrances of lovingly cooked meals. Until we cook again—happy slow cooking!

INDEX

YOU can get this ebook for free after sending me your name and email address.

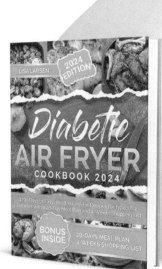

BONUS

Diabetic
AIR FRYER
COOKBOOK 2024

1700 Days of Easy, Healthy Low-Fat
Recipes for Type 1 & 2 Diabetes with a
28-Day Meal Plan and 4-Weeks
Shopping List

Lisa Larsen

GET THIS E-BOOK FOR
FREE

YOU can get this ebook for free after sending me your name
and email address.

✉ manychatarl@gmail.com

Made in United States
Troutdale, OR
12/10/2024

26279682R00053